Taking the Lead

Published by

Featherstone Education Ltd
44-46 High Street
Husbands Bosworth   Lutterworth
Leicestershire LE17 6LP

First published in the United Kingdom, October 2005
ISBN 1 905019 37 8

British Library Cataloguing in Publication Data.
A catalogue record for this book is available from the British Library.

Featherstone
Education

Printed in the UK on paper produced in the European Union from managed, sustainable forests

Taking the Lead

Managing Effective Provision
for Families and Young Children

Pat Brunton and Linda Thornton

Featherstone Education

The manager is responsible for bringing practitioners from a range of different backgrounds together to achieve results for children and young people that could not have been achieved by any one of the agencies acting alone.

Toolkit for Managers of Integrated Services (2005)
www.everychildmatters.gov.uk

Contents

Introduction

Taking the Lead **examines the different aspects of management which are key to the successful delivery of integrated services for young children and their families.**

Although the core skills of management in any organisation are similar, the examples used here are set in the context of managing childcare, early education and family services within the evolving framework of Every Child Matters: Change for Children. The particular benefits and challenges of managing multi-agency teams made up of professionals from diverse backgrounds are recognised, as are the advantages and realities of successful partnership working.

The content covers the six areas of expertise defined within the Common Core of Skills and Knowledge for the Children's Workforce, in particular those relating to multi agency working.

Chapter 1 looks in detail at the **planning process** and how to address it in a step by step way, starting with an analysis of your vision and values. It ends with a review of the purposes and importance of good monitoring and evaluation.

Chapter 2 reviews the skills you need as a **team manager**, looks at the characteristics of an effective team and considers the challenges of effective partnership and inter agency working.

Chapter 3 highlights the importance of **professional development** and looks at ways to manage a training and professional development programme which benefits both the organisation and the individual members of your team.

Chapter 4 explores **managing quality** through developing effective policies to cover all aspects of your services. It looks at the stages in writing a policy, provides an example of the key issues which a policy might address and provides a standard format for a policy document.

Chapter 5 deals with **management of time**. It looks first at some techniques for reviewing your use of time and then suggests a number of strategies for getting the most out of time spent in meetings.

Chapter 6 considers aspects of **financial management** including budget planning and monitoring and the importance of having in place sound financial policies and procedures.

Chapter 7 focuses on a key aspect of **people management** - how to make sure that you recruit the right members to your team to deliver your development plans effectively. It looks at induction procedures for new staff and the benefit of having an effective appraisal or performance management system in place.

Chapter 8 examines ways of **getting to know your customers better**, so you can look at how you tailor the services you provide to suit their needs. The final section of this chapter - Creating Your Image - encourages you to look again at the corporate image you want your organisation to present to the local community and the wider world. Re-examining your vision and values takes you back full circle to the strategic planning process discussed in Chapter 1.

What makes a good manager?

Managing an organisation that delivers a wide range of services is an exciting, but challenging and demanding role. To achieve this successfully these are the main skills and dispositions you will need:

Strategic vision and lateral thinking
Being able to see the big picture and how initiatives link together, support and complement one another.

People management
An ability to manage the delegation of responsibility and develop the skills of individual team members.

Empathy
An appreciation of a range of different perspectives, seeing the strength in different arguments and being open to possibilities.

Communication
Enthusiasm and passion for the job and an ability to communicate ideas to a wide range of audiences.

Financial awareness
Good budget management skills underpinning an ability to make money work as effectively as possible.

Legal astuteness
An understanding of what is, and is not, legally possible and the confidence to make this known to people, individually or collectively.

An eye for detail
An awareness of how to maximise opportunities, look for gaps and overlaps and minimise duplication of services or funding.

Flexibility
An outgoing, open minded approach which is receptive to new ideas and new ways of doing things.

Enthusiasm for change
A willingness to take time to talk to people, find out what they think and why they think it, and what they would like to change.

Professional robustness
An ability to shrug off the inevitable misunderstandings and misinterpretations which are part and parcel of team working.

While this list may appear daunting at first sight, personal reflection on your individual characteristics and aptitudes will help you to decide which aspects of management you are already proficient in, and which areas could form the focus for your own professional development.

This book will provide you with the strategies and information to help you develop the necessary complement of skills, knowledge and attitudes to be a successful manager of integrated services for families.

Chapter 1

Planning, Monitoring and Evaluation

An understanding of strategic planning is one of the key skills a good manager can bring to the organisation they are responsible for. The strategic plan, and its careful monitoring and evaluation, provides the framework for all the other management functions that you are responsible for.

This chapter looks in detail at the planning process - who you should involve, how to define your vision and values, understanding where you are now, identifying where to go next and working out how you will get there. The final stage of the process - deciding how you will know when you have arrived - involves looking in some detail at the purpose and importance of monitoring and evaluation.

Planning - why do it?

'To fail to plan is to plan to fail' (Anon)

Strategic planning, at its simplest, involves deciding where you want to go and what you want to do, and then creating a route map in order to get there.

The planning process can be time consuming and labour intensive, but it is important to remember all the benefits it brings to your organisation.

A good strategic plan:

- demonstrates how your organisation will fulfil its aims, objectives and targets;
- acts as a form of communication to highlight potential links with other organisations, initiatives and services;
- demonstrates how funding will be used/generated;
- provides a structure against which progress can be monitored;

- helps individual members of the team see how their contribution fits in to the overall plan for integrated service delivery;
- enables team and partnership members to appreciate the 'big picture';
- provides information for parents, carers and other service users.

Who should be involved in your plan?

The wider the range of stakeholders you consult during the planning process the broader the range of options you will come up with for deciding on the detail of service delivery. To keep the process manageable it is important that the consultation process sets out the broad framework and terms of reference for future developments. This keeps everyone focussed and realistic and prevents effort being wasted on considering possibilities which at the end of the day simply don't fall within the remit of your organisation.

The following should all play a part in the planning process. Some will appear in the early stages, whilst others appear right through to the final stages of deciding the detail of actions, timescales and funding allocations:

- users of integrated services parents, carers and children in your local community;
- organisations and agencies which deliver services on behalf of your organisation;
- the management committee of your organisation;
- staff working at all levels;
- members of the local community, including elected representatives.

The planning process

Stage by stage, the planning process involves:

1. Knowing who you are
- defining your vision and values

2. Understanding where you are now
- analysing your strengths and weaknesses

3. Identifying where you want to go next
- reviewing the services you provide

4. Working out how you will get there
- defining your aims and objectives

5. Deciding how you will know when you have arrived
- monitoring and evaluation.

1. Knowing who you are

Central to your organisation will be the vision and values which define what you stand for and underpin all that you do. These will only be effective if they are shared by all the members of the team and are therefore best drawn up as a group exercise so that everyone participates and can feel ownership.

Vision

Your vision is a statement of what you are setting out to achieve and where you would like your organisation to be in three or five years time. For example, your vision for the future might include some of these:

- being an expanded service which caters for twice as many families;
- achieving quality assurance accreditation;
- all staff trained to NVQ level 3 or above;
- new premises with better facilities for parents to meet and study;
- a fully comprehensive information service for families.

A shared vision gives every individual member of the team and the wider organisation a better understanding of the part they play in achieving overall success. It also highlights the challenges that must be met in making your collective vision a reality. The vision of every organisation will be different, but there are common characteristics of an 'effective vision' which helps to guide the process. (Kotter,1996)

Imaginable: your vision conveys a picture of what the future might look like, in a way that other people can understand.

Desirable: it appeals to the long term interest of everyone involved in your organisation - customers, employees, institutional stakeholders.

Feasible: it incorporates realistic goals which are attainable.

Focused: it provides sufficient detail to help you in the decision making process - this keeps the vision firmly embedded in the day-to-day life of your organisation.

Flexible: there is scope for individual initiative to respond to changing circumstances.

Communicable: you can explain your vision easily, and can get your message across in five minutes.

Values

Agreeing and stating your values defines the philosophy behind your way of working and gives clear messages about what you believe is important.

For instance, do you value:

- a commitment to equal opportunities for all families;
- childcare and early education of the highest quality;
- a respect for cultural diversity;
- the creation of an environment in which adults and children learn together?

Sensitively handled, the process of agreeing your vision and values will be a very productive exercise, bringing out into the open the real issues which need to be addressed to enable you to move forward confidently as a team. It is an opportunity for everyone in the team to understand one another's roles better and to look at ways in which their working practices can be streamlined to increase efficiency. This is particularly important as more and more multi- agency teams are brought together comprising individuals with very different job descriptions, working practices and lines of communication.

Your shared vision and values will act as a consistent point of reference while you decide which competing priorities to put into action during the course of the planning process.

Having come to an agreement about your vision and values, you then need to translate these into practice by carrying out the next stages of the planning process.

2. Understanding where you are now

A well-accepted way of carrying out an audit of your organisation, and working out where you are now, involves the use of a technique known as SWOT analysis. SWOT provides a simple and useful framework for undertaking an analysis of your current situation, its strengths and weaknesses and the opportunities for further development.

The SWOT analysis involves asking questions of your organisation and range of services under four simple headings, as in this example.

Example SWOT Analysis Questions

Strengths

What skills do the team have?

What experience do individuals bring?

What local partnerships have been created?

Which projects are already successful and can be built on?

Weaknesses

Which skills are missing from the team?

Is there an area of expertise/ experience which we lack?

Have we spent time on teambuilding and professional development?

Are all our policies up to date?

Opportunities

What funding opportunities are available?

What socio-economic or demographic changes in the local community are we aware of?

What new partnerships or networks could we create?

Threats

How can we ensure sustainability of new projects?

What socio-economic or demographic changes in the local community are we aware of?

Will Government policy change soon?

Strengths and **weaknesses** are internal factors relating to the organisation of your team and the delivery of the services you currently provide. Try to be realistic about these so you can see clearly what strengths can be built on and what weaknesses can be addressed - through better organisation, training or making new appointments.

Opportunities and **threats** are usually external factors relating to local and national initiatives and funding opportunities. These include shifts in government policy and economic, demographic or social changes.

Carrying out a SWOT analysis is a very useful exercise at the start of any planning process. If it is done initially as an individual exercise with the findings then shared as a group, it provides an interesting insight into different people's perceptions of your organisation. These views can often then become the focus for team building and staff development events in the future.

3. Identifying where you want to go next

This involves taking a closer look at the services you currently provide and evaluating how far individual initiatives and activities are fulfiling the aims originally set out for them.

Four categories you might come up with are:

Those **activities that are going very well and have reached or even exceeded the targets set for them** - You may want to look in your strategic plan at ways of developing these further - extending hours of opening, numbers of childcare places, range of family learning programmes etc. To help you plan future developments spend some time analysing why these activities have been successful so you can target your efforts more precisely in the future.

Good, consistent projects which provide the 'backbone' of your integrated service and continue to deliver at a steady rate year after year - An example might be high quality early education provision for children aged 3 to 5 years of age. Look behind the management of these projects to find out why they continue to perform well and be aware of any internal or external threats which may affect their smooth running.

Projects or initiatives which have had their day - ideas which, although they seemed good at the time, never came to fruition. Again try to work out why this happened: wrong time? wrong place? wrong target audience? ineffective management? poor quality? lack of communication? This information will be vital in informing future planning.

Possibilities - initiatives and ideas which have yet to prove their value. How long can you give them to deliver their targets? How can you help them along to give them every chance of success?

4. Working out how you will get there

Aims and Objectives

Once you and your colleagues have completed the stages outlined above, you will be in a strong position to agree your strategic aims and develop a series of precise objectives which will form the basis of your detailed operational or action plans.

> **Aims** state in broad terms what you would like one aspect of your integrated service provision to achieve.

> **Objectives** break these aims down into areas which are clearly stated and measurable.

For example, from all your analysis and discussion you may have agreed the following aim:

> **'That all parents will have access to high quality childcare and early education services that fit with their patterns of employment.'**

To turn this aim into reality you will need to break it down into a series of clear objectives which are SMART:

Specific - clear, concise and understood by the whole team

Measurable - so you can check on progress

Agreed - 'owned' by everyone, rather than imposed

Realistic - challenging but achievable

Time limited - to be achieved by an agreed date

An example of a SMART objective to achieve the aim set out on the previous page would be:

By the end of the financial year:
to have carried out a consultation with parents on their childcare needs; identified the key areas for development; and completed an action plan detailing how these services will be developed from April onwards.

This states clearly what is to be done, has a framework against which progress can be measured and sets a date for completion. Your strategic plan will be made up of a manageable list of aims each with a set of SMART objectives which set out what must be achieved. Each of these objectives will have a cost estimate attached to it to ensure that your planning stays firmly rooted in reality.

The next stage in the process is to define exactly what action must be taken in order to achieve the objectives.

Action plans

This level of planning includes the detail of all the different actions which will be carried out in order to achieve the aims and objectives of the strategic plan. It will include information on who is responsible for carrying out the actions, the timescale and the agreed budget allocations. The final information to include on the action plan is the detail of who will monitor the progress of the action and how they will do this. The importance of monitoring and evaluation is discussed in detail in the next section.

The table overleaf shows the first stage of action that should be completed to fulfil the aim and objective defined above.

5. Deciding how you will know when you have arrived

Monitoring and evaluation go hand-in-hand with planning in helping you make judgements on how well your plans are progressing and how well you are achieving your aims and objectives.

Monitoring describes the process of collecting data during the course of any project or initiative while **evaluation** refers to the analysis of this information to make a judgement on progress.

The actions planned out below relate to the aim on page 18 and the objective on page 19.

Activity	Who is responsible?	Who will carry it out?	Start date	Finish date	Cost (including source of funding)	Who will monitor progress?	How will progress be monitored?
Production of questionnaire	Childcare coordinator	Development worker	Sep 06	Nov 06	£500 (core funding)	Manager	Questionnaire: Trial of Questions
Completion of questionnaire	Development worker	Childcare and early education staff	Nov 06	end Jan 07	£250 (core funding)	Childcare coordinator	Completion of questionnaires by 60% of current service users
	Childcare coordinator	Childcare coordinator	Feb 07	end Feb 07	------	Service Manager	Weekly update on progress

A blank printable version of this Action Plan proforma is available on the CD ROM that accompanies this book for planning in your own setting.

Monitoring

Deciding on the information needed to monitor any particular initiative should be done at the time you are compiling the detailed action plan for that initiative. This is the time when you will be defining your objectives and agreeing the targets you hope to achieve. During this process it will be evident that there is certain information you can collect which will help you build up a clearer picture of the progress you have made.

The information you collect will come in two forms:

Quantative - involving numbers and other statistical information

Qualitative - involve comments, notes and records of people's responses and impressions

Sometimes the monitoring plan can seem an extra task, on top of all the activity which needs to take place to fulfil the plan you have created. However, unless you agree the range of monitoring data needed at the beginning of the project and decide how you are going to collect this information on a regular basis, opportunities will be missed and your evidence base for demonstrating the effectiveness of what you have done will be incomplete.

Having decided what you are going to monitor, remember the importance of collecting the baseline data right at the beginning of your project. Unless you do this you won't be able to evidence where you started from and will find it difficult to show that your action has had an effect.

The terminology associated with monitoring can occasionally cause some confusion. As well as the qualitative and quantitative data described above, you may also come across the terms **output** and **outcome**.

Output	Outcome
Refers to the direct results of activities. For example, the number of new 'wraparound' childcare places created.	Describes changes in socio economic or physical conditions. For example, the increase in the percentage of single parents in employment.

The outputs achieved by your project may eventually translate into outcomes, or they may not.

In the example on page 18, the availability of childcare at the beginning and end of the day may make it possible for more single parents to work. This presupposes that suitable employment opportunities exist in your local community. If they do not, then extending opening hours will have no effect on local employment statistics.

Effective monitoring helps you to keep an eye on the progress of your initiatives and helps you to decide on any small changes you may wish to make which will improve efficiency and effectiveness.

Evaluation

In contrast to the 'day to day' collection of data involved in the process of monitoring, evaluation takes a longer term view of the progress of an initiative or project and sets out to answer the important questions, such as:

- how effective an activity is in delivering the aims and objectives set out in the original plan;

- how cost effective it is;
- what impact it is having.

Evaluation can be carried out at different times during the course of a project, as a final evaluation, as an interim evaluation part way through, or as part of a rolling programme of evaluation.

Each of these types of evaluation serves a different purpose. Choosing which evaluation protocol you use for any project depends on its nature, timescale, the range of organisations and personnel involved, and any requirements set out by the funders.

Final Evaluation

- Occurs at, or near, the end of a project or initiative.
- Is outward looking in that it providers information for beneficiaries and for the project funders.

- Asks whether the requirement for accountability and value for money have been fulfilled.
- Focuses on the impact of the project and the lessons which can be learnt by others.

Pilot projects trialing new ways of doing things, for example wraparound childcare provision, are generally subject to a final evaluation to establish the important messages to be carried forward in the roll out of the programme.

Interim Evaluation

- Takes place mid way through the life of an initiative or project.
- Reviews progress, suggests changes and identifies any further information needed.
- Contributes to the forward strategy for the project.

Interim evaluations will be a feature of any of the initiatives you are managing which run for more than one year. An example, might be a three year programme for the development of family support services.

Rolling evaluation

- Timetabled in to the project on a continuous basis, in a similar way to monitoring.
- Goes beyond monitoring in the analysis of information by looking at final objectives and outcomes, not just activities and outputs.

You may choose to carry out a rolling evaluation on any initiative which is new to you, and of particular importance to the success of your organisation. An example, might be a move into the development of childcare provision for children under the age of 3.

Some pitfalls to avoid when considering any evaluation of your project or programme are:

Dead weight - evaluation must not measure those changes what would have happened anyway

Double counting - activities should not be counted if they are out puts from other programmes

Why is evaluation so important?

The word evaluation derives from a Latin word which means 'coming from our values'. Knowing what the values of your organisation are, and what you are seeking to achieve, should provide the starting point for any evaluation process.

Like monitoring, evaluation can sometimes seem like an additional burden. It takes time over and above the organisation and delivery of activities designed to implement your plans, but to counter this it is worthwhile considering the benefits of evaluation from a range of different perspectives.

Benefits of evaluation for organisations and partnerships	Benefits of evaluation for staff
Helps clarify aims and objectives.	Provides feedback on performance.
Ensures that resources are used efficiently.	Challenges assumptions, but can also confirm impressions.
Provides evidence of impact.	Suggests areas to develop further.
Sets standards and provides quality control.	Provides access to the views of other members of the team.
Helps to validate new approaches, but may also uncover unexpected consequences.	Helps staff to see their work in a wider context.
Benefits of evaluation for the end users	**Benefits of evaluation for funders**
Provides information and an overview of the service being provided.	Helps to ensure the good use of funds.
Offers an opportunity to have their views heard.	Highlights good practice that is worth replicating.
Identifies any gaps in existing services.	Identifies gaps in existing provision.
Provides an opportunity for more active participation.	Informs future policy.

This chart is also available on the CD ROM that accompanies this book.

Finally, remember the role which the whole evaluation process can play in supporting the professional development of you and your team through developing analytical thinking and reasoning skills.

Monitoring and evaluation

Use these as starting points for discussion during a professional development/ teambuilding session.

Why measure performance?

- That which gets measured gets done.
- If you can demonstrate results, you can win public support (and funding).
- If you don't measure results you can't tell success from failure.
- If you can't identify success you can't reward it.
- If you can't reward success you are in danger of rewarding failure.
- If you can't see success you can't learn from it.
- If you can't recognise failure you can't correct it.

Why evaluation is good for you!

- It can help to develop your analytical thinking skills.
- It can help to foster logic and reasoning skills.
- It enables you to learn more about the work done by your colleagues in other parts of the organisation.
- It helps a wide range of stake-holders to learn more about your organisation and the integrated services it provides.
- It can help members of your organisation to see how the work fits in to a wider context.

Ten things to think about

1) Planning takes time, but you can ensure the time is used well if you approach planning in a series of sequential steps.

2) For planning to be effective it is important to involve all the key stakeholders appropriately.

3) The vision and values of the organisation must lie at the heart of the planning, monitoring and evaluation process.

4) Analysing your organisation in terms of 'strengths, weaknesses, opportunities and threats' will give you a clear idea of your current position.

5) Set objectives for development which are clear, measurable and time-limited.

6) Agree the monitoring plan at the same time as agreeing the action plan.

7) Define the data which will be collected and remember to collect the appropriate baseline information.

8) Be clear about who is responsible for collecting data, including the format and frequency with which it will be collected.

9) Choose an evaluation protocol which is appropriate for the type of initiative or project you are tracking.

10) The process of evaluation can be used as a very effective form of training and professional development.

Chapter 2

Managing Teams and Partnerships Effectively

As a manager you may well find that you have the responsibility to organise the smooth running not just of the team of people who work alongside you, but also of a wider partnership or management committee with distinctly different roles and responsibilities. This chapter looks first at the skills you need to achieve this - the ability to lead, motivate, instill trust and give praise and recognition, and at the characteristics of effective teams. The particular challenges associated with the effective management of partnership working are then looked at in more detail.

Managing a team

As the manager, you will have overall responsibility for delivering the services required by the organisation you work for, within an agreed time scale and budget allocation. To achieve this effectively a large proportion of your time and effort will be directed to managing a diverse team of people who have day to day, hands-on, responsibility for the activities of your organisation.

Effective team management requires you to adopt a wide range of roles relevant to different aspects of the job you are doing. Sometimes you will be the leader, at other times the motivator, from time to time the coach or mentor, but in all situations you will need to be a skillful and effective communicator. In this chapter we will look first at the requirements of each of these roles and then consider different aspects of recruiting, training and retaining a successful team.

Leading, motivating or mentoring?

'Leading by example - it's not the main thing, it's the only thing.'

As the leader of the team you have a responsibility to keep in mind the big picture, to be aware of the vision and mission of your organisation and the overall strategic plan. From time to time you may need to re-tell the story to remind people of how past actions shape current activities and define plans for the future. This role is particularly important when your organisation brings together team members from diverse backgrounds with different aims, objectives and aspirations.

The personal attributes of a good leader include:

self awareness

trustworthiness

optimism

flexibility

As a good leader you will be aware of the effect you have on others and the need to be a good listener - conscious of both the verbal and non verbal messages you receive from, and give to, the team you are managing.

In your role of 'manager as motivator' you have a responsibility to create an environment in which everyone understands their role, feels good about the work they are doing and wants to achieve their best. Individual members of the team will be motivated by different things. Good motivators spend time finding out what 'makes people tick' and what it is about the job they do which gives them the greatest satisfaction. This information can then help in planning future roles for team members, at the same time balancing the needs of the individual against the needs of the organisation.

From time to time, as a manager, you will find yourself taking on the roles of coach and mentor, delivering on the job training for members of your team. These are demanding roles which requires good personal organisation and self discipline, time and patience. To be successful you need to convey interest and enthusiasm, be clear when giving instructions, as well as being a good listener, and be able to give useful and constructive feedback.

All these different management roles rely very heavily on your skills as a communicator. Managing people well involves giving members of the team regular, objective feedback on how well they are performing; consulting and seeking opinions on future developments; and putting in place systems to share and disseminate information on how the organisation is doing. Periodically, it is useful to review the communication structures you use - e-mails, meetings, video conferencing, circulars, telephone calls, newsletters, reports and questionnaires - to check that they are still being used in the most efficient way and are achieving the purpose for which they were intended.

Creating and managing a team

A very simple way to assess how well you are currently managing your team is to ask yourself the following questions:

- are the members of my team happy?
- are they cooperative and keen to accept responsibility?
- are they rarely absent from work?
- is the quality and quantity of their work high?
- are projects completed on time?

In an ideal situation every member of the team will feel valued, respected for the contribution they make, and motivated to achieve their best both for themselves and for the organisation.

Team working doesn't happen by chance - a team is very much more than simply a group of people working together on the same project.

Take time to develop and nurture the effectiveness of your team and to develop a common understanding of shared goals and shared responsibilities.

The characteristics of an effective team

- Team members recognise that they are dependent on one another and that mutual support is the best way of achieving both individual and team objectives.
- Team members trust one another and make an effort to understand one another.
- Open and honest communication is a feature of the way the team works - the usefulness of constructive criticism is appreciated by all parties.
- There is an understanding that disagreement is inevitable, but that this can be used as a source of new and better ideas about how to do things.
- Team members support one another and iron out any differences of opinion or approach internally, within the team situation.
- Team members take corporate responsibility for achieving the aims, objectives and targets of the team.

Managing a partnership

The term partnership is used throughout to refer to a group of representatives brought together to oversee the development of a new organisation, initiative or project. Typically membership will be drawn from a range of different areas of the public, private and voluntary sectors - including parents, who will all have an interest and involvement in the development and smooth running of the new organisation.

Knowing how to work effectively with a partnership, and how to get the most out of everybody's time and effort, is therefore an essential managerial skill.

Different forms of partnership differ in the specific roles, responsibilities and accountability of the individual partnership members. In some instances membership is open to all, in others there are specific membership requirements designed to facilitate accountability to a broad ranging interest group. Many partnerships are made up of a mixture of service providers and service recipients, each with their own priorities and interests. In this section we will look at the common factors fundamental to the overall effectiveness of any partnership.

Why have a partnership?

Partnership working is not easy. Most partnerships make mistakes from time to time and all partnerships have to contend with challenge and change on a regular basis.

What then are the advantages of partnership working, which outweigh the disadvantages?

Partnerships are established, and sustained because they:

- link services together in a way that is more understandable and more accessible for the customer;
- provide better ways of accessing customers and finding out what they need.
- are a cost effective way of delivering services;
- improve the overall quality of the range of services provided;
- support participation and community involvement;
- build capacity for ongoing, sustainable development by raising the level of skills within the community.

A successful partnership requires time and effort and a great deal of commitment on the part of the key players. Remember, the characteristics of effective teams referred to earlier in this chapter apply equally well to partnerships.

A shared purpose and a common goal

Perhaps the most important, and often the most neglected, aspect of a partnership's role is an understanding of:

what it is?

why it exists?

what it is trying to achieve?

All partnerships bring together a diverse collection of individuals with different skills, experience, expertise and hopes for the future. This is their strength, but, unless recognised and developed, can also be part of their downfall.

For any partnership to work together effectively everyone needs to understand where everyone else is coming from and what their aspirations, and limitations, are. Bringing together a disparate group of individuals and expecting them to work together successfully from the outset simply will not work.

For any new organisation or initiative, and periodically for any established venture, time needs to be set aside to define, or reinforce, the vision, values and purpose to which everyone subscribes. Working through this process is the ideal opportunity to gain an understanding of the different views and ideals of the members of the partnership and to fuse these together into a common goal which you can all subscribe to.

Having a common purpose provides the glue which holds all the other parts together and increases mutual understanding and appreciation. It helps the smooth day to day running of any project, and is absolutely vital when the going gets tough. Think of those occasions when the partnership is faced with tough decisions on staff appointments or redundancy, on funding, on new initiatives, or on the handling of complaints from dissatisfied customers - all regular aspects of the work of any dynamic and forward looking partnership.

Effective partnership members

The ideal partnership is made up of representatives of all the interest groups served by the organisation you are managing.

These representatives understand:

- what high quality provision for young children looks like;
- the remit of all their fellow partnership members;
- legal requirements and employment law;
- the value of time and funding for staff development.

These representatives are:

- willing listeners and skilled communicators;
- aware of the requirements and implications of the Children Act;
- aware of financial management regulations and audit requirements.

These representatives can:

- represent the views of parents and other service users;
- recognise the big picture and how they fit into it;
- keep up to date with the latest government initiatives affecting childcare, early education and family support;
- appreciate the importance of appraisal and performance management.

These representatives have:

None of us can hope to achieve all of these attributes as individuals.

- delegated responsibility to make decisions on behalf of the organisation they represent;
- have an in-depth knowledge of the local community.

Good partnership management therefore relies on sensible delegation of responsibilities, good leadership, effective chairmanship and, above all, trust.

Communication and Consultation

Communication and establishing a culture of information sharing is crucial in the early stages of partnership development. Ignorance, or lack of awareness, can unnecessarily extend the early stages of partnership formation. From the outset the partners need to learn as much as possible about each others roles and responsibilities in order to come to a common understanding about how each can contribute to the partnership.

Information is power - shared information is shared effectiveness.

Consultation, between partners, with the intended beneficiaries and with the community will be the keystone of making partnerships work. Consultation is a costly and time consuming process and should be planned carefully to ensure that the correct questions are asked, and that expectations are not raised which cannot then be fulfilled. The results of any well planned consultation exercise provide valuable information for partnerships on how they could reshape the services they provide. It is important that you feed back this information in an accessible way to the people who were involved in the consultation process so they can see that their comments have been listened to.

Time for partnership development

Partnerships are often formed to respond to a new initiative or to establish and run a new project or programme. In all instances there will be pre-determined targets to meet within a restricted time frame. The pressure will be on from the outset to get on with the job. However, experience of partnership working right across the public, voluntary and private sectors has shown unequivocally that the most effective and long lasting partnerships are those which invest time in developing the partnership itself.

As the manager, it is your responsibility to make sure the partners understand the importance of prioritising this process. Time is needed at the outset for the partnership members to establish a shared vision and to agree common values. Thereafter, regular reviews of partnership working will refresh and revive the partnership and help to keep pace with changing circumstances and working practices.

Responsibilities and management structures

Unless established as a separately constituted body, most partnerships will have one lead partner which will often also be the employer of the partnership staff and the route for channelling funding to the deliverers of partnership services. It is vital that the partnership manager clearly defines the roles and responsibilities of the partnership staff and that all members understand the day to day management structures within which the partnership staff operate.

The stages in partnership development

The classic description of the phases which any newly established team, committee or partnership go through have been described as:

Forming

Storming

Norming

Performing

Forming

At the early stages of establishing the partnership your main focus will be on determining which organisations should be represented in the partnership and by whom. A desire to be inclusive can have the inbuilt danger of creating a very large and diverse partnership which is not sufficiently focussed on the task in hand. Remember that partnership membership, like all other aspects of partnership working, should be open to regular review and change. Partnership decision making is possible only if representatives have delegated powers from their organisation to make decisions - be aware that this ideal may take some time to establish.

Storming

It is reassuring to know that virtually all partnership arrangements go through a difficult phase before they settle down to deliver the services they were set up to provide. The storming phase needs careful management, and shouldn't be allowed to continue for too long, but it should lead in the long run to better mutual understanding and more genuine partnership working.

By their very nature most partnerships have to face the challenge of distinguishing between the provider and purchaser roles among partnership members:

Provider refers to those representatives in your partnership who provide services, and are funded through the partnership to do so.

Purchaser refers to those representatives in your partnership who commission, or buy services.

Decisions involving allocation of funding to service providers should only be made by partnership representatives who do not have a financial interest in the outcome of the decision. As the manager you may find it useful to establish a smaller management group to make these decisions, made up of partnership members who are not direct service deliverers.

Norming

At this stage in the process the partnership will be agreeing its strategic and action plans, defining its evaluation strategy and contracting for the delivery of the services it intends to provide. This is the stage at which roles and responsibilities, policies and procedures, will come to the fore. Clear lines of accountability should be defined and, if necessary, sub groups or working parties set up to oversee particular aspects of the partnership's work. Regular reporting arrangements and arrangements made for collecting all the quantitative data needed for evaluation purposes should be agreed.

Performing

This stage, as its name suggests, is the phase of partnership working when it will appear to the observer that most activity is taking place. This in no way diminishes the huge amount of time and effort you as the partnership manager will already have invested in moving the partnership on to this stage. Ideally, the partnership will remain in this phase until the task for which it was set up is complete, but as circumstances and priorities change it is sometimes necessary to revert, albeit briefly, to the storming phase in order to move initiatives on.

Joining, staying and moving on

As a manager you will be aware that finding, and then retaining, good partnership members is vital for the smooth and efficient running of your organisation. When looking for new members you will want them to feel confident that they have the time, skills and expertise to make a useful contribution. A regular audit of the skills and experience of the existing partnership will help to show where the gaps are and enable you to target your recruitment efforts to fill these gaps. Individuals are much more likely to volunteer their services when they can see clearly the benefits their involvement might bring to the partnership as a whole. Then, to help them understand the big picture and how they fit into it, it is a good idea to put together an induction pack. This will provide an overview of roles, responsibilities and expectations, pinpoint essential information and where to find it, and also give a brief history of the organisation or project to date to provide a context for future actions.

Partnership members stay involved when they can see how common goals can be achieved, and future activities developed, that will be mutually beneficial. As projects evolve and change direction it is inevitable that some individuals will feel they no longer have a role to play and will become less active. Look upon this as success rather than failure. Every successful project, and every partnership, needs to respond to change and to move on in order to develop and grow.

Celebrate your successes, thank all concerned for their time and involvement, and then check your audit of skills to find out who you need to target next for your partnership.

The 5 Cs of effective teams and partnerships

Communication: knowing who to ask and where to look to find information.

Consultation: staying in touch with the users, both parents and children.

Confidentiality: having a clear understanding of information that can be shared in a wider arena, and what cannot.

Commitment: attending meetings and carrying out agreed actions.

Corporate responsibility: supporting the decisions agreed through the partnership process.

How effective is your teamwork?

This evaluation chart may provide you with a useful tool for evaluating how well you work as a team. Answer the questions yourself and ask members of your team to do the same. This will give you an overview of how the group as a whole perceives the quality of its teamwork and will help you make changes which ensure that the partnership progresses effectively.

We...	Always	Usually	Rarely	Never
have respect for the leader				
show respect to each other				
share the same values				
agree about principles				
know our importance to the organisation's success				
listen to each other				
value one another's strengths				
compensate for one another's weaknesses				
are willing to contribute ideas				
speak openly and trust one another				
compromise over disagreements				
bury conflicts once they are resolved				
are possibility thinkers				
adapt well to change				
learn and develop together				
solve problems creatively				
solve problems practically				
hold effective meetings				
meet our targets				
are budget conscious				
want to be working where we are				
want to be doing what we do				

A printable version of this chart is available on the CD ROM which accompanies this book.

Ten things to think about

1) Do you have shared goals that everyone in the organisation understands?

2) Do you value one another's contribution to the team/partnership?

3) Are all the members of the team or partnership encouraged to play an active role?

4) Do you invest enough time in developing the team/partnership itself?

5) How good are you at sharing and disseminating information?

6) Do you consult widely to take into account as many different viewpoints as possible?

7) Do you have agreed working procedures that we all stick to?

8) Are our decision making procedures transparent and understandable?

9) Do we have an up to date induction pack for all team/partnership members?

10) Do we celebrate success?

Chapter 3

Managing Professional Development

Updating your own skills and gaining new qualifications - by attending training courses, studying at home, studying as part of a distance learning programme, or by carrying out a work based research project - are all part of the professional development of a manager. Maintaining and developing the quality of the services your organisation provides involves investing time and money in ensuring all staff have access to the training opportunities they need to do their job well.

This chapter looks at the different types of training which individuals and teams need, how to get the most out of your training budget and ways of helping team members pass on their learning to colleagues.

Why do we need training?

Statutory requirements

Statutory requirements set out the basic qualifications needed by your staff in order to do their job successfully. At any one time you may have several members of staff engaged in work based learning - gaining the qualifications they need to fulfil the requirements of their post.

In addition, in childcare situations, staff teams need to have appropriate qualifications in child protection, child safety and first aid. It is worth noting a change in emphasis that has occurred in the national standards for day care. The terminology 'the designated person responsible for ...' has been removed and there is now a requirement to consider what training all staff need to give them the necessary skills in a particular field.

It may well be that you would wish to consider the benefits of a similar broadening of responsibility when considering the training requirements of your own staff team.

The Children Act (2004) introduced new legislation and statutory requirements which have training implications for staff at all levels of your organisation. For Managers of organisations providing integrated services for children aged 3 to 5 years, the Foundation Stage is now a specific phase within the National Curriculum and the six areas of learning covered in the Curriculum Guidance for the Foundation Stage are statutory. Early years practitioners have a responsibility to ensure that they have the skills, knowledge and understanding to plan, deliver and assess this phase of the curriculum.

For children with special needs the evidence shows that early identification and intervention provides the best long term outcomes. Staff teams who work with young children and families should include individuals with an awareness of special needs and disability, and an understanding of how to access professional guidance.

Professional competence

Over and above the statutory requirements, there are many areas where new initiatives and changing circumstances identify additional training needs. Depending on the nature of your organisation this could involve gaining an understanding of the Birth to Three Matters framework, advice on developing family learning programmes, working with families and children from ethnic minorities, or play provision for older children in out-of-school clubs. The Common Core of Skills and Knowledge for the Children's Workforce identifies six areas of expertise needed by professionals working with families and young children. This is the essential audit tool to use when identifying the training needs of your team.

Managing training

The scenarios described above clearly demonstrate the very wide ranging and diverse aspects of training and continuing professional development which you as a manager need to keep abreast of.

- are able to access the training they need;
- achieve a balance of time between that spent on training and that spent at work;
- feel that they are being treated fairly;

- recognise that there is an appropriate split between the development needs of the individual team members and the development needs of your organisation.

This involves ensuring all staff:

Staff induction procedures and annual reviews of performance, appraisal interviews or performance management meetings all provide useful opportunities to review the training needs of individual members of your staff team (see page 84). These can then be formally agreed and timetabled over the coming year. Feedback from training and an analysis of the effect it has had on personal performance becomes part of the annual review cycle.

In addition, your strategic and action plans detailing the areas for development for the organisation over the coming year will identify training needs and opportunities for the staff team. Deciding how these requirements will be met, and by whom, helps to focus the training budget on areas of the greatest importance and helps to ensure that statutory requirements are covered.

Facilitating professional development

Encourage a positive attitude to professional development by picking up on staff interest in courses and training opportunities - for the benefit of the organisation and for themselves.

Keep up to date with training opportunities in your area and further afield - through local networks and organisations, your Early Years Development and Childcare Partnership (EYDCP) and Local Authority training programmes, information from Further Education (FE) and Higher Education (HE) institutions, information about government initiatives in fliers, newsletters, adverts and websites.

Make sure you are on the e-mailing list for newsletters from appropriate organisations - these are often a good source of information about training activities or resources available either free, or heavily subsidised.

Be aware of funding possibilities - through government initiatives, European Funding, EYDCPs and Learning and Skills Council initiatives to promote skills development.

On some occasions it may be possible for two individuals from your organisation to attend a training event together. This can be very valuable, and is often a good way of supporting reluctant participants, who can then share ideas and experiences and plan for change together. From time to time you may want to arrange for your whole team to attend the same training event, giving you the best possible foundation for effecting change and moving your practice forward.

Cascading training

Provide opportunities - time and resources - to enable staff who have attended training to feed back to their colleagues and share what they have learned. This is a great way to focus the mind during a training event; the discipline of reflecting on learning in order to explain it to someone else helps to consolidate understanding.

Not everyone in your organisation will find this easy - staff need opportunities to gain the skills they need to become good trainers themselves. Staff will need access to ICT equipment and training, plenty of opportunities to practise their new skills, and helpful advice and feedback from colleagues. Start small to build confidence and allow colleagues to develop their skills over time.

Be aware of the whole range of skills and training that is required for organisations, and the individuals working in them, to be effective. These include not only professional competencies, management, leadership and teamworking skills, but also training which helps individuals cope with the scope and challenges of the job - the balance of work with personal life and the management of stress are areas which spring to mind immediately.

Broadening the scope of training

Professional development is not always about individuals going on training courses. Distance learning, individual study and research, and well planned and structured action research are all equally important. All these activities, if carefully planned to fit with your organisation's aims and objectives, will contribute to ongoing development and progress.

Finally, don't forget your own personal and professional development needs. Make sure you have a training plan, and a training budget allocation, alongside everyone else and use your skills and experience to set an example as the 'lead learner' in your organisation.

Ten things to think about

1) How do you ensure that all staff meet the statutory requirements of their position?

2) Does your induction procedure identify the training needs of new staff members?

3) Do you use annual reviews of performance as an opportunity to review the training needs of individual team members?

4) Do your action plans identify areas and budgets for staff development?

5) Do you have a training plan, and budget allocation for the whole organisation?

6) Have you identified who is responsible for managing this plan?

7) Do you encourage individuals to develop their own skills as trainers?

8) Do you provide the time and facilities for individuals to pass on their training experiences to colleagues?

9) How well do you access external funding sources to stretch your training budget?

10) Do you make good use of opportunities to provide training for other local organisations and colleagues?

Chapter 4

Managing Quality

As a manager you have responsibility for ensuring the quality of the wide range of integrated services your organisation provides. All aspects of the organisation contribute to the quality you provide - the people, the premises, the standards of care, teaching and learning, and relationships with parents and the local community. The most effective way to manage this responsibility is to develop a range of policies relating to these areas which can then be used to ensure a consistent approach.

This chapter looks at the stages in writing a policy, provides an example of the key issues which a policy on inclusion might address and provides a standard format for a policy document. It looks at the benefits of achieving a quality assurance award.

How do policies support quality?

Policies are descriptions of principles, expectations and procedures. Anyone reading your written policy will know what has been agreed on any specific issue, and will know what they, or anyone else, is expected to do in particular circumstances. Policies are what give any organisation its coherence and help it to present a well organised, consistent image. There are some policies which you must have by law. Examples of these include health and safety, child protection, equal opportunities and staff employment. Over and above this, you will want to draw up a range of policies which enhance the quality of your provision and show how you will put your vision and values into practice. These may include policies on staff appointments, teaching and learning, working with parents and staff development.

Policies which are required by law

All practitioners need to be aware of the legislation which affects children's lives and sets out the minimum requirements which must be met by law. Every organisation will have a series of policies which set out how these legal requirements are going to be met on a day to day basis. You may find that model policies are available from your Local Authority, your EYDCP or your professional organisation. You might choose to adopt a model policy as it stands. This will help you to ensure that you comply with legislation. However, as your organisation will have its own identity and ethos, you may prefer to use a model policy as a basis for discussion and to provide the framework for producing your own policy statement.

Writing policies

Policies might be written by the manager, the management group, the staff of the organisation, or by small working groups. In all cases the most effective polices are drawn up following consultation with a wide cross section of interested parties.

Policies are there to give clarity and consistency about how your organisation operates, telling everyone what to expect and what is expected of them. You should make your policies known to, and understood by, everybody. In some instances this will involve looking carefully at the language you use in your policy document, and the way you present it, to make sure that it is accessible and understandable.

A policy is not meant to be fixed in stone or to prevent things from happening! Rather, it should be enabling and empowering for the staff who are expected to implement it.

Stages in writing a new policy

All new policies should reflect the values, vision and ethos of your setting. To achieve consistency you will find it useful to have a structured approach to creating policies, similar to the one outlined below.

1. Preparation Stage

- The manager and senior staff research the background information for the area which the policy will cover.

- They identify the key features to be included in the policy and how best to put them into practice.

- Any training needs are identified and addressed.

- Key stakeholders are consulted on the proposals and the results are analysed.

Questions to ask:

- What is happening in your organisation now?
- Who does what?
- Who has been on relevant training?
- Where can you find out about good practice?

- Are there any statutory requirements?
- How can you find out?
- Who can you talk to?
- Who are the key stakeholders?
- How will you consult them?
- What is the timescale?

2. Writing Stage

- Using the information from the consultation process, a few people draw up the policy together.

- Use a simple standard format for your policy document. (see the opposite page)

- State who is responsible for seeing the policy is implemented.

- Define the action which has to be taken.

- Decide how the policy will be monitored.

- Make sure the policy is freely available and well publicised.

Questions to ask:

- What does the consultation tell you?
- Do you need to change anything?
- Who will write the policy?

- Will you use a standard format?
- When will it be written?
- Are there any training needs?
- Who needs to know about the policy?

3. Review Stage

It makes sense to review your policies periodically to make sure that they are still appropriate. You could draw up a three year plan for reviewing policies so that you are not under pressure to look at everything at the same time.

Sometimes you may need to change a review date because of circumstances such as a change in the law or a decision that has a knock-on effect.

Questions to ask:

- Has the policy been fully implemented?
- Has it been monitored well?
- Does it contribute to quality provision in your organisation?
- Do you need to make any modifications?
- Has it achieved its aims?
- Is it compatible with your other policies?

Keep your policies as short and as clear as possible. You might want to support them with additional information and reference material as appendices. Lengthy documents take a long time to produce and are less likely to be read, understood and acted upon.

A Sample policy - Inclusion

This example illustrates the way in which a well written policy can support high quality practice throughout your organisation.

A policy for inclusion should meet all the legal requirements of the statutory frameworks but should go beyond this to encompass the spirit and not just the letter of the law. Inclusion should not be the responsibility of just one member of staff, but should include everyone - the fundamentals and principles which underpin good practice in providing for children with additional needs are identical to those which apply to all children.

The following information should be included in your policy:

- a clear statement about what the policy is trying to achieve and how it relates to statutory legislation;
- the name of the person responsible for coordinating day to day provision for children with additional needs;
- the support which the setting can provide including any special arrangements to improve access;
- arrangements for regular monitoring and evaluation of the effectiveness of provision;
- arrangements for partnership working involving parents, carers and, where possible, the child;
- a procedure for handling comments and complaints.

From policy to practice

To bring your policy on inclusion to life the following organisational aspects will need to be considered:

Providing information and support for parents

Effective communication with parents is fundamental to the early identification, assessment and support of children with additional needs or disabilities. Parents need to feel that their views are valued and to know that confidentiality is respected. They need information in a form that is understandable and the reassurance that there are experienced individuals with whom they can share their concerns and anxieties.

Training for all staff

To support early identification and effective inclusion it is vital that all staff, not just the Special Educational Needs Coordinator (SENCO), have a good understanding of child development so that they can identify children with additional needs and provide the appropriate support to address those needs.

Partnerships with other professionals

Spending time fostering links with other professionals improves the ability of your staff to provide for the children for whom they are responsible as well as furthering their own professional development. In addition, it creates a vital link and support structure for families.

Record keeping and transfer of information

To ensure that the benefits of early identification and intervention are not lost, it is important to build up good partnership arrangements between the setting which a child attends before the age of five and the school to which the child will transfer. This is a two way process involving accurate and concise record keeping on one hand, coupled with a willingness to value and respect the information which is passed on.

Quality Assurance

There are many different quality assurance schemes to choose from to enable you to demonstrate the value you place on providing quality services. Some, such as Investors in People, focus on the organisation and how well it values and uses the skills and talents of its workforce. Other quality assurance schemes assess the quality of the services provided, particularly the extent to which they go beyond any statutory requirements.

Achieving a quality assurance award can demonstrate effective teamwork, motivate staff, provide a valuable marketing tool as well as being a cause for celebration for all involved.

A standard format for a policy document might include:

Title:...

Date adopted by the management group:..................

Person responsible:..

Introduction
(Why do we need this policy? What is its legal status? What background information do we have? How does it reflect our vision and values?)

Aims and objectives
(How do these relate to our setting's vision, aims and quality issues?)

Roles and responsibilities
(Who does what?)

Action to be taken

Who will be responsible for monitoring?: ....

How will they monitor?

Date for review:..

This policy document template is on the CD ROM that accompanies this book.

Ten things to think about

1) Policies give any organisation coherence and help it to present a well organised, consistent image.

2) There are some policies which you must have by law, and several others which will assist the smooth running of your organisation.

3) The most effective policies are drawn up following consultation with a wide cross section of interested parties.

4) Policies need to be accessible and understandable to all.

5) Ensure new members of your team are fully aware of the range of policies your organisation has.

6) Be clear about who has responsibility for implementing different aspects of any policy, and how this will be monitored.

7) You will find it useful to have a structured approach to writing policies to make sure they complement one another.

8) Create a rolling programme of policy review to make sure individual policies are accurate, appropriate, and in keeping with current legislation and good practice.

9) Use your policies as evidence of the quality of the services your organisation provides.

10) Stand back periodically to make sure you can find good evidence of policy into practice.

Chapter 5

Managing Time

Managing a demanding job, with wide ranging responsibilities, while at the same time maintaining a reasonable work-life balance, can sometimes seem an impossible task. Good organisation of time and space will make a significant contribution to your long term success, especially when you are trying to cope with the trials and tribulations of establishing new initiatives and managing fast moving, diverse projects and programmes.

This chapter looks first at planning your use of time and then focuses on ways to make the most of time spent in meetings. It reviews the purpose of different types of meetings and outlines some strategies for making meetings as effective as possible.

Effective time management requires discipline - both from you and from the team who work with you. Even the best time management structure will fail if you don't stick to it, and ensure your colleagues also understand and respect it.

One of your personal goals will probably be to avoid the stress caused by an ever increasing number of urgent tasks building up, none of which you feel able to tackle effectively, because you are too busy worrying about the things you haven't done.

Ultimately what you will aim to do is to minimise wasted time and maximise quality time spent either individually or as part of a team, carrying out the various aspects of your management role. Members of your team need to understand that timetabling the times of the day or week when you are available to them increases, rather than decreases, the quality of your involvement.

Don't forget the vital contribution an attractive, well organised, uncluttered office environment makes not only to your efficient use of time but also to your physical and emotional well being.

Reviewing your use of time

As a first exercise you will find it interesting, and revealing, to think carefully about how you structure your day.

Try asking yourself the following questions:

Do I prioritise my day, or does it just happen?

Do I know the value of my time?

When considering distribution of work load, and opportunities for delegation of tasks, it is useful to think about the comparative cost of your time, and that of members of your team. You may then decide that there are some routine tasks that it is simply not cost effective for you to perform.

How often do I use a time log?

This requires self discipline as a time log needs to be kept over an extended period - a week or a fortnight - in order to provide useful information. Analysing the log, and calculating the percentage of your time spent on different tasks will help you to review how this time breakdown fits with the key duties and priorities set out in your job description. Regular, perhaps twice a year, use of a time log will help you to keep track of changing work patterns and should encourage you to be realistic about how many new responsibilities you can take on without delegating some of the old ones.

Analysing your use of time

Once you have gained a better understanding of how you currently use time, you are in a position to look at ways you might want to change your routine to make it more efficient, and more effective.

Check through your time log and group the tasks you do under the following three headings:

Category A tasks: tasks which are urgent and important;

Category B tasks: those which are either urgent, or important, but not both;

Category C tasks: routine - neither urgent nor important.

To help you organise your time effectively, you now need to plan a realistic selection of tasks from categories A, B and C for one day. Try to spread these throughout the day to give yourself a good balance of activity. The time at which you do different things will depend on your personal working style - are you at your most effective first thing in the morning, or do you take a while to get going?

The secret is to keep a balance between the different categories. If, at the end of this exercise, you find your schedule is full of Category A tasks you are running the risk of putting yourself under too much pressure. Think about either redefining some of these tasks or delegating them to someone else.

Using a time planner

The particular time planning system you use is a matter of personal preference. It could be either paper based or electronic, but the important thing to remember is that there must be only one - many of us fall into the trap of trying to run two parallel systems, and then have to face up to the inevitable embarrassing consequences.

Consult your diary at the beginning of each day to review the category A, B and C tasks you have planned. As you work through these it is always satisfying to cross them off as they have been achieved. At the end of the day you will find you have added several new items. Prioritise these as category A, B or C tasks and plan them into your work schedule accordingly.

Delegation

As the manager, all new initiatives, action plans and tasks to be completed will come to you first before they are passed on to the rest of your team. As the paperwork comes in you will be regularly reviewing the roles and responsibilities both of yourself and your team, and dividing your management tasks into:

- **- those which only you can do;**
- **- those which require input from others;**
- **- those which can be delegated.**

The benefits of delegation include not just freeing up more of your time, but, provided the right tasks have been delegated to the appropriate individuals, delegation also increases staff motivation and job satisfaction.

The key here is to delegate a range of tasks - those which are enjoyable as well as those which are routine.

Remember, things which you find tedious may be fascinating to another member of your team with a different personality, interests and experience. Successful delegation depends on you knowing your team well and making sure that sufficient time and resources are made available to help them complete the tasks you have delegated. This may initially require extra time input from you, but the rewards will come in the form of team development and, very importantly, succession planning. If you don't delegate tasks and responsibilities there is considerable danger that the organisation will be 'back to square one' should you decide to move on to another post.

Why have meetings?

As a manager you may find that up to half of your working week could be taken up with meetings of various kinds. Maximising their efficiency will make a major contribution to keeping the demands of your job under control.

The question 'Why having meetings?' must occur to you every time you look at your diary for the week and see one meeting after another timetabled in. Plenty of time for talking about things, but precious little time for getting on and doing them!

Meetings are an important form of communication, but it is useful from time to time to take a step back and ensure your time, and that of your colleagues, is not being wasted.

To do this you need to:

- be aware of different types of meetings;
- understand the purpose of the meeting and consider alternative ways of communicating;
- devise strategies to make sure meetings are effective in terms of both time and outcome.

Types of meetings

The most frequent type of meeting in your working week will involve one person, or a small group of people. These may be formal and well defined, focusing on specific issues, or may be less well defined and more general in nature. In terms of overall time management for you as a manager you might like to consider setting aside a regular time slot when staff can book meetings with you. This avoids the 'have you got a minute' scenario where you find yourself constantly interrupted, but still ensures that your staff know you are available to them.

Some small meetings, such as staff appraisal, have a well defined purpose, structure and time scale which should be adhered to by all parties. For small meetings of a more general nature it is good practice to agree an agenda and timescale either beforehand, or at the start of the meeting, and to ensure that issues are dealt with in priority order.

Larger meetings require considerable advance planning and take up a considerable amount of time - before, during and after the meeting. From time to time it is worthwhile looking at the cost effectiveness of meetings of this type to ensure that you have not fallen into the trap of holding them simply out of habit. Perhaps there are other forms of communication you could use which are equally effective, or perhaps even better?

Large meetings - what's their purpose?

Having a clear understanding of the purpose of any large meeting you arrange will help not only to make it more efficient, but may indeed suggest ways in which the issues could be handled differently, avoiding the need to hold the meeting at all. Taking a broad overview, large meetings are held for the following purposes:

To impart information
Training events, conferences and workshops are good examples of meetings designed largely to impart information. Their timing and structure reflects this, although it is important to schedule in time for delegate feedback in order to retain them as active participants in the process.

To exchange information and make decisions
Communication in this type of meeting is a two way process as it relies on the expertise and experience of all those who attend. It is vital that everyone feels involved, and sees that they have a role to play.

To build relationships between working colleagues
This could be both within an organisation and between organisations and agencies. This aspect of meetings is one which isn't always considered, but is crucial to the success not just of the meeting, but of the whole organisation or project you are managing.

When you are thinking about organising a meeting consider first whether other forms of communication - telephone calls, video conferencing, newsletters, questionnaires, e-mail discussion groups or distance learning materials would be equally effective.

Strategies for making meetings effective

Timing and frequency of meetings

How often do you need to meet? For everyone's benefit it is useful to agree a timetable for meetings. This will depend upon the purpose for which the group meets together, and the speed of change with in the organisation.

- Aim to achieve a balance between keeping people informed and allowing time for activity to take place.
- There will never be an ideal date or time that suits everyone but try to be inclusive by varying both the day of the week and the timing during the day so that no organisation or individual is repeatedly prevented from attending.
- Agree a calendar of meetings at least six months, and preferably a year, in advance while people's diaries are relatively empty.

Venue and attendance

- Choose a venue that as many people as possible can access easily. Be aware of equal opportunities and your obligations under the Disability Discrimination Act.
- If a representative is unable to attend a meeting they may wish to send a 'named substitute'. In this instance make it clear that the substitute will be expected to have all the paperwork and background information relating to the meeting they are attending.
- Remember that not everyone who attends your meetings will be in salaried positions within the organisation they represent - paying transport and childcare expenses may be appropriate.

Setting the agenda

This is the vital ingredient which gets the meeting off to a good start and gives you the best opportunity to ensure that time and energy is used effectively.

- Try to send the agenda out at least a week before the meeting to act as a reminder for people to attend.
- Set a deadline of 10 to 14 days before this for people to send in items they wish to be included on the agenda - this helps to keep everyone involved and avoids meetings becoming a one way process.
- Make sure all background paper work is sent out with the agenda.
- Use standard items to introduce (apologies for absence, minutes of previous meeting etc.) and close (date and time of next meeting) each meeting.
- Structure the agenda to prioritise items in order of importance.
- Suggest approximate timings for items to be discussed.
- Indicate on the agenda if an item is for discussion, or simply for information.
- Have an agreed strategy for 'Any other business' (A.O.B.) - use this for information items only and insist that items which require discussion are carried forward to the next meeting.
- Set a start and finish time for the meeting - and stick to it!

Managing the meeting

It is important for one person to act as the chair and take responsibility for the overall management of the meeting. In addition somebody should be appointed to take a set of notes to act as the minutes of the meeting and a record of any decisions reached.

To make the most effective use of everyone's time the chair should:

- start the meeting on time;
- not waste time re-visiting the last meeting in detail;
- assume that everyone will have read their background paper work - do not waste valuable meeting time going through the detail of this;
- manage the time taken to discuss agenda items fairly, so that items are given the time and attention they deserve;

- agree which, if any, items are confidential. Keep these to an absolute minimum, but be aware of the legal framework in which your organisation are operating;
- manage representatives with a lot to say and encourage less forthcoming members to express opinions, perhaps by asking them directly for their views;
- at the end of a reasonable period of discussion, summarise the points raised and ask for agreement on a decision;

- make sure the wording of the decision states what is going to happen, who is going to do it, and what the time scale will be;
- ensure the wording of this decision is noted exactly - if necessary re-read it and revise it until everyone in attendance is in agreement;
- remind everyone of the date and time of the next meeting;
- close the meeting at the agreed time and thank everyone for their attendance.

After the meeting

- Send out the minutes as soon as possible after the meeting.
- Put names against particular items in the minutes to remind people what they agreed to do.

- Start to prepare the agenda for the next scheduled meeting.

Assessing your time management skills

Use the time management review document in the table below to highlight the areas in your time management that you need to address.

	Never	Occasionally	Frequently	Always
I make a list of things to do every day.				
I open my mail as soon as it arrives.				
I skim read relevant newspaper and magazine articles.				
I read internal memos as soon as I receive them.				
I read internal memos thoroughly later.				
I keep my in-tray under control.				
I consider carefully who needs the information I am circulating.				
I clear my desk at the end of each day.				
I arrive on time and am prepared for meetings.				
The meetings I organise finish on time.				
The meetings I organise achieve their purpose.				
I achieve a balance between thinking time and action time.				
I decide how many times I can be interrupted in a day.				
I close the office door when I do not want to be interrupted.				
I reserve certain times for visits from colleagues.				
I am able to complete tasks without interruptions from colleagues.				
I allow a colleague or secretary to screen my telephone calls.				
I limit the length of my calls.				
I tell telephone callers that I will return their call, and do so.				
I delegate tasks to colleagues that I could do myself.				
I follow up on delegated work.				
I make sure I know about the latest information technology.				
I keep my computer files in order and up to date.				

This time management review document is on the CD ROM that accompanies this book.

Meetings - how well do you do?

In order to review how effective your meetings are, encourage your team or partnership members to fill in a formal assessment. There's a suggested template below. Try completing the assessment as individuals, then discuss your findings as a group. It will tell you a great deal about different people's perceptions and provide a good starting point for reviewing the way that you work. An exercise like this often highlights problems of communication and understanding, which can then be addressed.

	Never	Sometimes	Usually	Always
We plan meetings well in advance.				
We vary the times/dates of our meetings.				
We start our meetings on time.				
We finish our meetings on time.				
Everyone can contribute to the agenda.				
The agenda is clear and self-explanatory.				
All paperwork is sent out at least a week in advance.				
I read the paperwork before a meeting.				
We use the item 'Matters Arising' appropriately.				
We have an agreed policy for 'Any other business'.				
We are clear about how to treat confidential items.				
We have clear expectations of courteous behaviour.				
Our decisions are made clear and we all abide by them.				
Minutes are distributed within 10 days of the meeting.				
We take action as agreed in the minutes.				
We are clear about delegated responsibilities.				
Our meeting room is user-friendly.				

This meeting review template is on the CD ROM that accompanies this book.

Ten things to think about

1) Good organisation of time and space will make a significant contribution to your long term success.

2) Effective time management requires discipline - both from you and from the team who work with you.

3) Regular use of a time log will help you to keep track of changing work patterns.

4) Successful delegation depends on you knowing your team well and giving them time and resources to complete the allocated tasks.

5) It is useful to have an understanding of the hourly cost of every member of your team.

6) Understanding the purpose of different meetings will help you think about alternative ways of communicating.

7) Agree a calendar of meeting at least six months ahead, while people's diaries are relatively empty.

8) Choose a meeting venue that as many people as possible can access easily - be aware of equal opportunities, and your duties under the Disability Discrimination Act.

9) Set the meeting agenda carefully - it gets the meeting off to a good start and ensures you use everyone's time effectively.

10) Get the most out of the meeting by utilising the skills of the chair and the minute taker to the full.

Chapter 6

Managing Money

Controlling the finances of your organisation is central to your role as an effective manager, and will include one or more of the following aspects of 'money management':

- preparing a financial management plan as part of your strategic development plan;
- setting an annual budget;
- monitoring your budget monthly;
- reviewing financial policies and procedures.

The total budget for which you are responsible will vary, as may the degree of flexibility you have in allocating spending, or generating additional income, but the same underlying principles of financial management apply in all cases.

Good financial management is the key to the successful development of new initiatives as well as to the maintenance and expansion of existing activities and programmes.

This chapter reviews financial management planning, budget planning and budget monitoring and the importance of establishing sound financial policies and procedures.

Financial management planning

Managing money well enables you to turn your ideas into reality and is therefore reliant on the production of a well thought out development plan which is sufficiently detailed to allow accurate costings to be made. Although you may feel that managing money takes up a lot of your time, this is time well spent, especially in the early stages of a project. Without sound financial procedures in place, and a good ongoing understanding of your budget, even the best intentions and innovative initiatives run the risk of not succeeding - failing to plan is planning to fail.

Financial management plans, or business plans, are put together at the beginning of a new initiative and reviewed regularly thereafter as the project develops. As they gather together all the important information you need to develop your project, they act as a road map detailing the expected route you intend to take to develop your project.

Planning in detail, including realistic estimates of costs, makes you think through any new developments in advance and raises the questions that have to be answered in order for your project to succeed. Once you have this information you are then in a position to change direction, take a detour, slow down or speed up as circumstances dictate.

When putting together a financial management plan it is often helpful to separate your costs into two categories - start up costs involved in getting the project going and running costs associated with keeping it running on an annual basis.

The individual areas of expenditure will vary depending on the nature of your project, but are likely to include most of the following:

Start up costs

- personnel costs in advance of the project opening;
- equipment, including office equipment and telephones;
- utilities - gas, water and electricity;
- supplies and resources;
- advertising costs;
- professional and legal fees and insurances;
- payroll and bank expenses.

Running costs

- salaries;
- accounting costs and payroll expenses;
- rent;
- supplies and resources;
- office expenses, including telephones;
- utilities – gas, water and electricity;
- repairs and maintenance;
- transport;
- insurance and advertising costs;
- training and professional development;
- depreciation;
- contingency reserve.

Financial plans should run for a minimum period of three years, with year one planned in detail, and outline plans for years two and three. Plans for projects which rely on grant funding to cover initial start up costs need to demonstrate how ongoing running costs will be met once the period covered by grant funding has ended. This could be either through income generation or through accessing alternative sources of grant or mainstream funding.

Ignoring this issue at the time of starting out on a new project greatly increases the risk of the project failing two or three years down the line due to lack of robust financial planning.

Budget planning

Once the funding for your organisation or project has been secured the annual budget available will be known. This funding can then be allocated against distinct budget headings to create a balanced budget for the year.

Achieving a balanced budget plan, where total allocated expenditure matches the income available, often calls for a number of adjustments and recalculations.

It is a good idea to retain all this information to enable you to see at a later date how the final figures on the budget plan were arrived at. This helps you to check that there are no gaps or double counting in the expenditure plans.

Remember that your budget plan is there to enable you to carry out the detailed proposals contained within your project development plan. The two should be closely linked, and if possible cross referenced, to make it easier for you to see where you might need to make adjustments to expenditure during the course of the year.

Budget monitoring

Regular, preferably monthly, budget monitoring is essential to keep track of expenditure and to make sure spending stays on course. This can be done by using a standard computer based financial management package or by writing the information on a spreadsheet.

Typical headings on a monthly spreadsheets detailing expenditure are:

Area of expenditure	Budget	Committed	Remaining	Comments

At the stage of drawing up your budget plan you will have given careful consideration to the itemised areas of expenditure you set up. These need to be broad enough to draw together similar types of expenditure under one heading, but still be sufficiently detailed to allow you to track spending. Experience over the course of the first year will show if you have got this right or not.

The second column, the allocated budget for that area of expenditure, remains the same throughout the year.

Column three details the expenditure committed on a cumulative monthly basis, and is sometimes also expressed as a percentage of the original budget allocation.

Column four indicates how much money there is left to spend, again sometimes expressed as a percentage of the original figure.

The final column enables you to note down the reasons for any variations in expenditure - overspends that will be corrected or potential underspends that need to be re allocated.

When you look in more detail at the individual headings in your budget plan it will be evident that there are different spending patterns during the course of a year. Salaries, for example, are paid monthly, electricity or gas bills will be quarterly and spending on resources and equipment may happen twice a year.

To keep track of budget commitments and take into account these different patterns of expenditure you may want to set up a budget profile which indicates how much of the total budget allocation you expect to be spent at the end of each month.

Financial policies and procedures

Good financial policies and procedures are vital to the success of all organisations. They are there to increase the efficiency of the organisation, ensure funding is spent appropriately, and protect individuals from the risk of serious mistakes.

As a manager you may be part of an established organisation with its own financial management structures and working practices. In this situation it is your responsibility to ensure that you are aware of these regulations and understand how they affect the team you manage. You have a duty to implement them fully and to keep existing and new staff up to date and fully trained.

If you are setting up a new venture from scratch you will need to establish a financial policy suitable for your organisation.

Aspects which should be included within this policy are:

Areas of responsibility

- who can authorise expenditure;
- what level of expenditure different members of the organisation can authorise;
- who is responsible for authorising and paying invoices.

Day to day control structures

- who is authorised to place orders;
- responsibility for checking goods received;
- management and maintenance of stock.

Reporting systems

- the structure for tracking expenditure;
- the frequency of budget reporting;
- the detail to be included in reports.

Use the checklist for Financial Standards opposite to review the operation of your organisation and ensure that you have all the necessary financial safeguards in place.

Financial policies, like all your other policies, should include input from and be known to all members of the staff team. Making your approach to financial management transparent and consistent will avoid problems and misunderstandings. You will then be able to fulfil your responsibilities with confidence and ensure that you can be fully accountable for the budget which you hold.

Financial Standards

Aspect	Yes	No	Action
Are the responsibilities of the management committee, the manager and staff clearly defined and the limits of delegated authority established?			
Does the budget reflect the organisation's prioritised objectives?			
Is the budget subject to regular, effective monitoring?			
Does the organisation have sound internal financial controls to ensure the reliability and accuracy of its financial transactions?			
Is the organisation adequately insured against exposure to risk?			
If computers are used for administration purposes is the organisation registered under the Data Protection Act?			
Is all the computer based data protected against loss?			
Does the organisation ensure that purchasing arrangements achieve the best value for money?			
Are there effective procedures for the administration of personnel matters?			
Are all stocks, stores and other assets recorded, and adequately safeguarded against loss or theft?			
Is all income identified and all collections receipted, recorded and banked promptly?			
Does the organisation properly control the operation of bank accounts and reconcile bank balances with accounting records?			
Does the organisation control the use of petty cash?			
Are voluntary funds administered as rigorously as public funds?			

This financial standards assessment chart is also available on the CD ROM that accompanies this book.

Working within best value

Being aware of best value will assist you when making decisions about how money is spent in your organisation, and will help you to make good use of the funds you have available.

Why not consider drawing up a best value policy and continually challenge yourselves to stick to it?

The key principles of best value

The 'four Cs' of best value are:

Challenge

Consult

Compete

Compare

Think about how you might use the four Cs in the management of your organisation by considering the following statements:

Challenge

- We question why we do things.
- We are open to change.
- We have high expectations of everyone.
- We set challenging targets for improvement.
- We expect high standards from all.

Consult

- We provide clear information about the organisation.
- We consult on major changes and financial decisions that will affect the organisation.
- We actively seek a wide range of opinions on our work.
- We keep people informed of the results of consultation.

Compete

- We have robust financial procedures to get the best service at the best price.
- We monitor customer satisfaction with services, particularly those which are charged for.
- We make financial decisions in the best interests of the children and the parents.
- We regularly investigate alternative sources of supplies and services.

Compare

- We use a wide range of data to compare our organisation with others.
- We expect to perform well when compared with similar organisations.
- We aim to ensure that all decisions on spending are made with a view to cost effectiveness.

Ten things to think about

1) Time spent on managing money well helps you to turn your ideas into reality.

2) Preparing a sustainable financial management plan will raise the questions you need to answer in order for new developments to succeed.

3) Budget plans and development plans need to be closely linked and cross referenced.

4) Monthly budget monitoring is essential to make sure expenditure stays on course.

5) Reviewing budgets periodically enables adjustments to be made to avoid underspends and ensure the overall budget for the organisation is used effectively.

6) Make financial awareness and an understanding of budgets a part of the induction and training programme for your team.

7) Use the principles of best value - challenge, consult, compete and compare - to test your financial planning decisions.

8) Good financial policies increase the efficiency of your organisation by helping you to keep track of day to day commitments and spending.

9) Good financial policies ensure that funding is spent appropriately.

10) Good financial policies protect individuals from the risk of serious financial mistakes.

Chapter 7

Recruiting New Members to Your Team

Fundamental to the effective and successful running of any organisation are the individuals who make up the staff team - each with their own talents, experience and expertise. As the manager, you have overall responsibility for ensuring that this staff team functions well and that the right people are recruited to join the team as vacancies occur or new posts are created.

This chapter looks at the different stages of the interviewing and appointment process - from advertising to shortlisting, to interviewing and appointing. Induction procedures for new staff are discussed and the value of performance management or appraisal systems are reviewed.

Should we have a recruitment policy?

As with any other policy, a policy on recruitment has the advantage of setting out a clear procedure which guides everyone involved through the process. It gives consistency, provides a realistic timescale, sets out individual roles and responsibilities and helps to avoid costly mistakes. Most importantly, it helps to ensure that recruitment procedures adhere firmly to all the requirements of current employment law.

Which position are we advertising?

When you lose a valued and respected member of staff your first thought may be to try to replace like with like. Remember that when a position becomes vacant you are in an ideal position to review the strengths and weaknesses of your existing staff team, assess current roles and responsibilities and look at different management structures. Only after you have gone through this process are you in a position to really know which job it is you want to advertise.

Who do we want to attract?

Qualifications and experience will be of fundamental importance and will form the core of the description of the post you are advertising. In addition there will be certain personal qualities which you may be looking for in potential applicants to complement your existing staff team.

One interesting way of defining individual skills and attributes involves the use of the descriptions proposed by Honey and Mumford (2001) which describe how different people approach problems and challenges. In their analysis of staff teams they defined four groups of people:

Activists
Reflectors
Theorists
Pragmatists

Activists

Activists like to be involved in new experiences. They are open-minded and enthusiastic about new ventures, but get bored with implementation.

Reflectors

Reflectors stand back and look at a situation from different perspectives. They like to collect data and think about it carefully before coming to any conclusions.

Theorists

Theorists adapt and integrate observations into complex and logically sound theories. They think problems through in a step-by-step way.

Pragmatists

Pragmatists are keen to try things out. They want concepts that can be applied and tend to be impatient with lengthy discussions.

Depending on the vacant position, and the composition of your existing team you may be looking for an Activist, Reflector, Theorist or Pragmatist.

The recruitment process

Advertising the post

If your organisation has clearly laid out guidelines regarding job adverts, these should be adhered to, but you may find that you have some scope to decide where it is most appropriate to place your advert. It is essential, in the interests of fairness, that all vacancies are advertised, whether internally - on a staff notice board for instance - or externally in a newsletter, in the local newspaper or in a national publication. Job adverts are expensive and it is essential that you include the correct information as clearly and concisely as possible to successfully attract potential applicants .

Use this checklist to make sure that the advertisement includes all the information needed:

- the title of the position;
- a very brief description of why your organisation is good to work for and what opportunities the post provides;
- an indication of the responsibilities of the post;
- any essential qualifications needed;
- the nature of the position - full time or part time, temporary or permanent;
- the salary range;
- a contact name, number and address;
- closing date for reply and, if possible, an interview date.

If you are placing an advert in a local or national newspaper, find out when it will appear and set your deadlines for responses accordingly.

Information for candidates

Having fully reviewed the vacancy before it is advertised you will be able to produce a concise, up to date, job description which defines the responsibilities of the post. Be realistic about how many different areas of responsibility you include on this - 12 is manageable, 20 is too many. Group these in order of priority so that candidates can address their letter of application to the specific areas of responsibility which the position entails. This should be accompanied by a person specification which describes the personal qualities and attributes you are looking for. Some of these will be essential and others desirable. Be very clear about how you divide attributes up between these two headings. At the shortlisting and interview stage you can't change the goalposts and decide that something which you put down as essential is in fact desirable, or vice versa.

You will also need an application form and some relevant background information about your organisation. Don't forget that the information you send out will give potential applicants a first impression of your organisation and should be carefully put together to reflect the image you want to convey.

To gain a first impression of the applicants to help you at the shortlisting stage, ask candidates to send you a written letter of application - be clear about whether you want this handwritten or typed - demonstrating how they feel they fulfil the requirements of the advertised position. This puts the onus on the applicant to address the specifics of the position you have advertised, rather than simply reproducing a standard application letter.

Shortlisting and inviting candidates for interview

If your advertising has been successful you will have received a large number of applications from which you now need to select the most suitable for interview.

Ideally the shortlisting should be carried out by the same group of people who will be involved in the interview process. In all instances candidates for interview should be selected on the basis of the information supplied in the application form and how well they match the person specification. Shortlisted candidates should be contacted by letter to confirm interview times and arrangements. References should be sought for each of the candidates to be interviewed. You will need to decide in advance whether you wish to take up references in advance of interview, and inform shortlisted applicants accordingly.

Be realistic about the number of candidates it is possible to interview in a day and schedule in regular breaks for the interview panel - the last candidate to be interviewed deserves as good a deal from the panel as the first.

If you want the candidates for interview to complete a task during the interview - make a brief presentation perhaps - provide all the necessary information about this in your letter. Tell them the subject you would like them to cover, the length of time they will be allocated and the equipment that will be available for use.

Unsuccessful candidates deserve an acknowledgement of their application - this will reflect well on your organisation, and you may well need to call upon their services in the future.

Interviewing

The interview panel will have been involved with the earlier stages of the appointment process and will have a good understanding of the nature of the post they are seeking to fill. The panel should come together at least half an hour before the first interview to agree the questions to be asked and who will ask them. These should be the same for each of the candidates, although particular themes can be explored through follow-up questions. In many instances it is helpful to draw up a grid on which members of the interview panel can record their notes and observations. When the whole interview process is completed these should be collected and kept as a formal record of the process.

To get the most out of the interview situation every effort should be made to help the candidates feel at ease. Interviews should start and end on time and the panel should be aware of the areas, largely relating to equal opportunities, in which it is inappropriate to ask questions.

If you have asked the candidates to make a presentation for a specific length of time, make sure that they stick to this so that you can make an honest assessment of one candidate's performance against another.
At the end of the interview the candidate should have the opportunity to ask any questions they may have. They should then be told when the decision will be made and how they will be informed of whether or not they have been successful.

Finally it is worthwhile checking that the candidate is still interested in the post and confirming that you have the correct contact information. Remember to thank each candidate for all the time and effort they have put into their application.

Making a decision

At the end of the whole interview process the panel will be in a position to make a decision about which candidate seems the most suitable for the post. The information they have at their disposal will come from the candidate's application form, letter of application, responses to interview questions, any verbal or written presentation during the interview, and possibly the references provided by previous employers. When all this information has been reviewed and assessed there will, hopefully, be one candidate to whom you wish to offer the post. If the panel members agree that there is also a suitable alternative applicant this should be noted, in case your first choice declines the post. Informing the successful candidate is easy, talking to the unsuccessful candidates will require all your skills of tact, diplomacy, empathy and honesty. It is a good idea if the interview panel agree the reasons that will be given to the unsuccessful candidates so there is a clear corporate understanding of why decisions have been made. Remind the interview panel of the confidentiality of all discussions and be sure to collect in all paperwork - application forms, candidates letters, references, interviewers notes and comments - for safekeeping.

If in doubt...don't!

Advertising and interviewing is an expensive and time consuming process, but making an unsuitable appointment is far more costly in the long term. If you are unsure it is better to face up to the prospect of going through the whole appointments process again.

Getting off to a good start

Having gone through the interview and appointment process it is important that the successful candidate gets off to the best possible start as a new member of your organisation.

Think about the following:

- Does the successful candidate have all the information they need about the post they have accepted?
- Do you have a well planned induction programme to bring new members into your team?
- Does your induction pack contain up to date information about policies, procedures, health and safety guidelines as well as organisational and procedural details?

- Are new employees given appropriate on the job training to help them understand their roles and responsibilities?
- Do you arrange a follow up interview with new staff to gain their initial impressions and then use this information to improve your induction procedures?

A good induction process will lead to more effective communication, greater motivation and quicker productivity.

Keeping things running smoothly

- Is information freely available within your organisation (within previously agreed confidentiality policies)?
- Do you regularly review your communication structures to ensure they remain appropriate?
- Are employees consulted on future plans, and are they able to see the results of these consultations put into effect?
- Do you periodically take time out to concentrate on developing the effectiveness of the team?

- Do you have an appropriate performance management/ appraisal system in place, which is understood by all, and allows your staff to comment on how well they are managed.
- Are your employees able to access appropriate training to enable them to do their job effectively?
- Do you have a robust and fair policy on personal professional development?

Performance management or appraisal

Performance management or appraisal are terms used to describe a regular planned cycle of appraisal and review meetings which helps all individuals in a team understand how they are performing in relation to the shared, agreed goals of the team and the organisation. The performance management cycle involves three stages, which take place over the course of a calendar year.

Stage 1

A performance management meeting is held between the team member (appraisee) and the team leader (appraiser). At this meeting the aims, objectives and targets of the organisation are reviewed briefly in order to set the context for the individual's contribution towards achieving these. Progress is reviewed, often including a discussion of any self review documents which the individual may have completed prior to the meeting. Objectives for the coming year are discussed and agreed by both parties and a monitoring plan is established showing how progress towards the targets will be tracked over time.

A vital part of the process is the identification and agreement of any training or professional development needs that may arise from the actions planned for the coming year.

At the end of this stage of the process the two parties formally agree the performance objectives in writing.

Stage 2

This stage usually takes place over a twelve month period and focuses on the implementation of the monitoring plan agreed at the first meeting. Information is gathered and work shadowing takes place as agreed. It may be useful to plan an interim review meeting part way through the year to review progress to date.

Stage 3

At the end of the year a review meeting is held at which both the team leader and the team member can formally review progress made against the agreed objectives over the course of the past year. Reasons for achievement, or non achievement, of objectives can be analysed and discussed and progress with professional development can be reviewed. New objectives, monitoring programmes and professional development plans can then be made for the coming year, all linked to the aims, objectives, strategic and action plans of your organisation. Once this has been completed the appraiser and appraisee begin at stage 1 in the next annual cycle.

A performance management cycle gives you an opportunity to keep in touch with progress at all levels of your organisation. It provides invaluable information to guide the organisation's planning process, gives a structure and rationale to planning professional development opportunities and allows you to address shortcomings in performance in a fair and honest way. Finally, it can be linked directly to incremental pay awards through a performance related pay policy.

Printable proformas for all three stages of this cycle are available on the CD ROM that accompanies this book.

The senior manager in any organisation does not have to be personally responsible for carrying out the performance review process for all members of staff. This is a responsibility which can be very effectively taken up by team leaders at various levels in your organisation. Perhaps the biggest challenge is to establish who will be responsible for your performance management review, if you are the senior manager in your organisation.

Moving on

The more effective you are in managing the team of people for whom you are responsible the more likely you are to achieve the goals of your organisation, within budget and on time. In the process you will have helped the individual members of your team to consolidate and develop their existing skills and to learn new ones. Inevitably current team members will then find themselves in a position to move on to take greater responsibility themselves, perhaps outside your organisation. Consider this a plus, not a minus. Reflect on the influence you have had on their personal professional development and be enthusiastic about the opportunity to bring new skills and experience into your team.

Ten things to think about

1) Having a recruitment policy helps you to ensure that your procedures adhere to the requirements of current employment law.

2) When a position becomes vacant, take the opportunity to assess current roles and responsibilities and to consider different team structures.

3) Make sure that your adverts include all of the necessary information and reflect the image of your organisation.

4) Spend time carefully preparing a job description, person specification and relevant background information to attract the right candidate.

5) Ensure the interview panel are clear about the position they are interviewing candidates for.

6) Plan the interview to cover all the essential aspects of the job description.

7) Review all the available evidence, including references, before coming to a decision.

8) Remember that interviews are a two-way process and all candidates should be treated fairly.

9) Plan your induction procedures carefully to get your new team member off to a flying start.

10) Use a robust performance management/appraisal system to link individual goals and targets to the development plans of your organisation.

Chapter 8

Knowing Your Customers and Creating Your Image

Although market research and image are terms which are traditionally associated with commercial activity they are equally appropriate when considering the development and roll out of new services in all sectors. Marketing our services and defining our image is something we all have to do - at different times, in different ways, and to different target audiences. Marketing is an essential skill needed by managers involved in new initiatives and developments in integrated service delivery.

This chapter looks at how good market research can help to provide the information needed to plan and market new projects, how questionnaires can be compiled and how information is collected and analysed. The stages involved in creating an image for your organisation are then reviewed, along with the different approaches you might use to market this image.

Why do market research?

Starting up new services, or expanding existing services into new areas is a time consuming process, often involving the investment of considerable amounts of money. Before putting in all this investment you need to be as sure as possible that the venture will be successful and will become profitable within a reasonable time frame. The term profit is applied here in a very broad sense, and also includes those many ventures which are designated 'not for profit'.

For any service, or product, to be successful there has to be a market for it - somebody must want to use it, or to buy it. As the instigators of a good idea - perhaps the development of a new out-of-school club in the local village school, the conversion of the pre-school from sessional to full day care, or the on site provision of new facilities for children under 3, you will probably be convinced that the idea is a good one, and that everyone will be queuing up to use the services you want to introduce.

The reality can be somewhat different, and unless you take notice of that reality and use all the information available to do some accurate, in depth market research you run the risk of starting up projects which will at best not fulfil their potential, and at worst be expensive and disappointing failures.

What do you need to know?

The bottom line of market research is that you can never know too much about your customers.

No matter how good you think the service you want to provide is, if it isn't what the majority of customers want, it will not succeed in the long term. Spending time, effort (and money) on carrying out a focussed, carefully thought out market research project will help to:

- refine your ideas to make sure that they meet local needs;
- give you the information you need to help you plan the detail of the service you intend to provide;
- indicate a suitable time scale for development of the project;
- provide the supporting information for a well researched business plan;
- help you to gain the funding you need to get your project started;
- measure how well your service is meeting a defined need and what improvements you can make.

As with most successful initiatives, the more time you spend in the early stages of the project defining what it is you really need to know, the more focussed and cost effective your market research will be and the greater the likelihood of it providing you with really useful information.

Once you have thought your idea through you will have a clearer idea of where there are gaps in your current information, and which questions you need answered.

You will need to collect quantitative and qualitative data. Quantitative information will be easier to collect and to analyse but qualitative information will give you a more in depth understanding of behaviour and why people do things. In any market research project you will want to gather a mixture of both types of information

How to gather information

Once you have decided on the range of information needed to answer your questions, you need to work out the most cost effective way of obtaining it. Depending on your circumstances, and the nature of the project you are involved in, you will probably want to use a combination of the following:

Desk research

Focus groups

Face to face interviews

Telephone interviews

Questionnaires

Desk research is the easiest and cheapest to carry out, especially for the non specialist. It involves finding and analysing a range of information which has been collected for other purposes, but which contains facts, figures and opinions which are relevant to the questions you are investigating. Desk research will give you an overview of the current situation but remember to take care when drawing assumptions from it - it is unlikely to be completely transferable to the service, geographical area or population you are interested in.

Focus groups are made up of existing or potential users of your service that you bring together in order to ask them a series of questions to find out their opinions, likes and dislikes. Sometimes it is a good idea to think about providing a small incentive of some sort to encourage participants to join in. Focus groups require the use of a trained facilitator and therefore can turn out to be an expensive option.

Face to face interviews allow more time for in depth questioning to take place but must be well structured in order to achieve their objective. The interviewer has more control because they can respond immediately to comments made by the person being interviewed. The disadvantage of face to face interviews is that they can be costly, time consuming, of variable quality and difficult to analyse.

Telephone interviews are less expensive to carry out and can often be combined with postal surveys. The questions you ask need to be clear and simple and the interviewer should sound friendly but efficient and be skilled at recording verbal responses on a standard recording sheet.

Questionnaires are commonly used. They can give structure to face to face and telephone interviews as well as being used for information gathering through postal surveys. Well thought out questionnaires help you to collect accurate information in a way which is easy to analyse. The key is to construct your questionnaire carefully to ensure it provides you with all the information you need. This aspect is considered in more detail in the following section.

Designing and using questionnaires

The quality of the information collected through a questionnaire is entirely dependant on the design of the questionnaire and the questions asked. When you are designing a questionnaire you need to establish your objectives, and what you want to find out about your customers.

The advantage of using questionnaires is that the data collected is comparable - if 10, 100 or 1000 people answer the same question the only variable should be their response. To achieve this the questions must be clearly written and unambiguous so that they are always understood by the reader in the same way.

Types of questionnaire

Structured questionnaires tend to be used in large, quantitative surveys. They consist of a series of precisely worded questions in a particular order and incorporate pre-coded responses. For this reason they are easily analysed.

Unstructured questionnaires can be used in face-to-face and telephone interviews. They usually consist of a checklist of questions which the interviewer can explore in depth depending on the responses given by the interviewee. It is often difficult to analyse unstructured questionnaires because of the much broader nature of the questions asked.

Semi-structured questionnaires use a combination of the two methods above and allow you to collect statistical data along with background information on the reasons why parents and carers think or do certain things.

Types of questions

Question types fall into three categories:

Classification - age, gender, location, number of children
Behaviour - what people do
Attitude - people's perceptions of why they do things

Classification

This covers a standard range of information, often linked to well established systems for defining population demographics - gender, social class, occupation, locality.

Behaviour

Behaviour questions include, for example:

Do you ever...?
When did you last...?
Do you use...?

These questions require factual responses which record people's behaviour.

Attitude

Attitude questions include, for example:

Why do you...?
What do you think of...?

These types of questions look at the reasons why people do things. Attitudes can be measured on a sliding scale from 'strongly agree' to 'strongly disagree' or by using symbols such as happy and sad faces.

What types of questions should you ask?

Open ended questions that begin with who, what, when or why.... These types of questions identify attitudes and feelings, but are time consuming to analyse as every response will be different.

Closed or **prompted** questions. These are quicker to analyse but you have to know all the possible answers in advance to provide the respondent with the correct range of options to choose from.

Filter questions. These guide the respondent through the questionnaire and tell them where to go next on the basis of the answers they have given to earlier questions.

Things to think about when compiling a questionnaire

- Always keep the aim of your market research in mind. You are less likely to waste time asking irrelevant questions and, more importantly, you won't miss that one vital question you should have asked.
- Think about how the questionnaire will be used. Self completion questionnaires have to be as clear and unambiguous as possible so the respondent can complete them easily.
- When you are writing the questions think about the person who will be completing it and the possible answers they will give.
- Group your questions in a logical order so areas of information are all dealt with together.
- Try to make your questionnaire visually appealing so people aren't intimidated by it. Try using smiley faces or scales for measuring attitudes.
- Use plain English and avoid any terms such as pre-school which can be interpreted in a variety of ways.
- If you are asking sensitive questions such as income or age, consider using response bands, but make sure these bands do not overlap or the respondent will find it difficult to complete the questionnaire and processing will be inaccurate.
- Avoid hypothetical questions and questions with a negative in them.

Once you have completed the first draft of your questionnaire read it out loud to make sure it makes sense. Then try it out on a few people to see how easy they find it to complete. Ideally this will include a small sample from the target group you intend to survey. Use their comments to improve the structure and layout before launching into your major market research project.

Having completed your market research, and analysed the information it has provided, you are in a much stronger position to decide what to do next. You will now have a much greater understanding of your customers and will know how to modify your plans to ensure that your project has the best possible chance of success.

Creating your image

As part of the market research process you will have had the opportunity to think in depth about the nature of your organisation, the services it provides and the image you would like it to present to the wider world.

This image will be one which conveys a clear message about who you are and what you do. It involves bringing together your core values and services and expressing them in a way which reflects how you would like to be viewed by your customers.

During the planning process (see page 13) you will already have spent time agreeing and defining your vision and value - what you are trying to achieve and where you would like your organisation to be in three or five year's time, coupled with a clear statement about the values which underpin your agreed way of working. This vision and its associated values lie at the heart of the image you want to create for your organisation.

What you do - the services you provide

The services you provide, and the customers you serve, may at first seem very obvious. You will already have carried out some market research amongst existing and potential customers - parents and carers in your local community for example. Although parents, and of course children, represent the majority of your customers it is worth spending some time thinking about the full range of services which you provide, and all the potential customers you cater for.

For example as a Children's Centre you may provide or co-ordinate many of the following services:

- childcare for children aged three months to five years;
- early education for three and four year olds;
- before and after school and holiday provision for five to eight year olds;
- drop off and pick-up service
- healthcare information and services for families;
- ICT and basic skill straining for parents and carers;
- training for NVQ students;
- parents' information service including childcare information, training and employment opportunities, parenting support and adult basic skills signposting;
- Childminder Network drop-in centre;

- a base for the local childcare network;
- toy and resources library;
- mentoring support for local providers involved in Quality Assurance accreditation.

Each of these services will have different customers with different needs and expectations, all of which need to be taken into account when looking at your image.

Try listing your services individually and then looking at the target audience for each of the different aspects of your provision. This will give you a more rounded view of what you do and will help you to create an image which fully reflects your organisation's role.

How do your customers see you?

What sort of image do you want to create for your organisation?
- Professional, well organised, inclusive, friendly, committed to high quality?

Having reviewed and redefined your vision and values and the range of services you provide you are in a position to manage the organisation of your setting to achieve this.

But what do your customers think?

Now is the time to stand back and take a good look at how your organisation is perceived by your customers.

- What image do they currently have of you?

- What do they think of you?

- What do they say about you?

You can get some useful pointers by taking an honest look at how your organisation presents itself to the outside world. However the only real way to find out is ask the customers, children and adults - through surveys, questionnaires, discussion groups and informal conversations. This will tell you which aspects of your current image work, and which don't.

Remember that it is your customer's **perception** of your organisation which is important, not how well you as a manager think it works. If you find you are not getting your message across to your customers successfully perhaps you need to look at how you communicate at all levels.

Don't forget that the image your customers have of your organisation covers all aspects of what you do and how you present yourself to the world. Try completing the questionnaire, Living up to your image, below. This will give you some useful pointers about what you need to change in order to improve the overall image your organisation presents.

Living up to your image requires constant attention, regular review and honest appraisal. But as it is at the core of the quality service you endeavour to provide it is a great motivator and a focus for teamwork and cooperation.

Living up to your image

Aspect	Yes	No	Action
Do we know what our customers say about us?			
Do we have a logo or identity which is used consistently and gives a clear visual message about what we stand for?			
Do we market our services effectively?			
Is information freely available and user friendly?			
Is the telephone answered in a consistent manner, and are messages passed on effectively?			
Do the staff have access to all the information they need and do they feel fully involved and valued?			
Do we value comment and feedback and use it to improve the service we provide?			
How quickly and effectively do we deal with complaints?			
How well do we involve ourselves with our 'local community'?			
Do first impressions show clearly what we value?			

This questionnaire is also available on the CD ROM that accompanies this book.

Marketing your image

Having created your image and organised how to turn it into reality you need to look at how you let the wider world - and all your potential customers - know about you. There are many different ways to do this, some more expensive than others, and all requiring time and effort on the part of you and your team. However, good marketing and promotion is essential to the ongoing success and development of your organisation and shouldn't be overlooked. If parents aren't aware that you exist they won't be able to access your services.

Many organisations define themselves by thinking about their unique selling point or USP. This defines what makes you different from other providers of childcare services and family support services. Perhaps you offer extended opening hours, special facilities for children with disabilities, on site training courses for parents, family support advice or information on job opportunities and training. Your market research will have told you which of these services is important to a particular group of customers. The service can then be marketed to them as a reason for using the services your organisation has to offer.

Don't be afraid of spelling out to potential customers why a particular service you provide will be of benefit to them:

Clouds Out of School Club is open from 7.30am. That means you can drop your child off and still be at work on time.

Southbridge Children's Centre runs computer courses on site, which means that you can gain an ICT qualification while your child enjoys our nursery.

You may choose to allocate part of your annual budget for marketing and publicity to produce leaflets, newsletters, posters, adverts or a website. A logo which gives a clear visual message about what you stand for will help you to establish your identity and should be used consistently on all promotional material including badges, letterheads and stationery so it becomes well known and instantly recognisable. Websites are a useful way of keeping people informed about future events and activities, but need to be updated regularly to retain their value. Perhaps the design and maintenance of your website could become a project for one of your community groups.

Press releases are a good way of gaining some free publicity for your organisation and cultivating a good relationship with the local newspaper can be a worthwhile time investment. For maximum effect you will need to present your information clearly and succinctly - try using the 'Writing a Press Release' guidelines on the following page to help you organise your copy.

Finally, having expended so much time and effort in creating your image you will be aware of the importance of keeping it under regular review. Remember to research customer needs regularly and use this information to feed in to your next cycle of planning, monitoring and evaluation - back to Chapter One!

Writing a Press Release

FOR IMMEDIATE RELEASE

Contact:

Tel:

Mobile:

Fax:

E-mail:

Address:

Date:

TITLE
(Not too long. Eye catching. Linked to local or national initiatives?)

Include all the relevant details in the first paragraph in case your Press Release is shortened for publication.

Try to start with an unusual opening sentence - something that will make people want to read on. A quote from a parent or a child always works well.

When you're writing the Press Release think about it from the reader's point of view - what would they be interested in?

As part of your marketing strategy you will probably have a vision and values statement (approximately 50 words) which sums up what your project stands for. Try to incorporate this in each of your Press Releases.

Keep the sentences short and uncomplicated - no more than 17 words to a sentence.

Use double or 1.5 line spacing for the text.

Complete paragraphs on the same page.

Indicate when you have come to the end by using:

###

Ten things to think about

1) Good market research provides the information needed to plan and market new initiatives - you can never know too much about your customers.

2) Spend time in the early stages of a new project defining what you really need to know.

3) Choose the most appropriate way of gathering the information you need.

4) A well written questionnaire is easy to analyse and will give you the information you need.

5) Clarify and define your vision and values to form the core of your image.

6) Review the range of services you provide and identify the customers you serve.

7) Stand back and look at your organisation from the customer's point of view - how well do you translate policy into practice?

8) Define your unique selling point and draw up a marketing strategy.

9) Make full use of press releases and similar opportunities for free publicity.

10) Regularly ask for customer opinion and be prepared to change in response to this feedback.

Conclusion

Successful multi agency and partnership working is the key to the development of effective integrated services for families and young children. This places demands on the manager of the organisation which are broad and far reaching.

This book has been structured to help you consolidate your understanding of organisational management and to recognise the wider challenges of leading and managing integrated services. Meeting the challenge of multi agency working to fulfil the remit of Every Child Matters: Change for Children has been recognised by the DfES as a priority area for development. Support materials for managers and aspiring managers are currently being developed and are beginning to appear on the Every Child Matters website (www.everychildmatters.gov.uk). You will find these provide a useful resource to supplement the information in this book.

Taking the lead can be used:

* to give an overview of the range of areas involved in managing integrated service provision;
* as a starting point for reviewing and auditing existing structures and systems and identifying your priorities for development;
* as a tool to promote shared understanding and support the management of change in your organisation;
* to help you prioritise areas for personal professional development.

Sources of information

Common Core of Skills and Knowledge for the Children's Workforce (2005) Every Child Matters: Change for Children. DfES/1189/2005.
Downloadable from www.everychildmatters.gov.uk

Curriculum Guidance for the Foundation Stage (2000) QCA/00/587

Birth to Three Matters DfES (BIRTH): available from DfES Publications 0845 6022260.

Children Act 1989: available from The Stationery Office 0870 600 5522 or downloadable from www.opsi.gov.uk/acts/acts1989

Children Act 2004: available from The Stationery Office 0870 600 5522 or downloadable from www.dfes.gov.uk/publications/chilrenactreport

References

Kotter, J.P. (1996) Leading Change. Harvard Business School Press. Boston.

Honey and Mumford (2001) Campaign for Learning. www.campaignforlearning.org.uk

What's On the CD

The CD ROM which accompanies this book contains copies of the forms and templates referred to in the text. These versions can be printed off and/or used in their electronic form. They are in Microsoft Word format, allowing them to be edited and adapted to suit your needs. The page numbers indicate which part of the book each item relates to.

Other publications for the Early Years by
Featherstone Education

First Hand – making the Foundation Curriculum work ISBN 1 902233 54 9
First Hand – new audit & policy framework ISBN 1 902233 55 7
First Hand – new audit and policy framework (CD) ISBN 1 902233 56 5
by Sally Featherstone

First Hand takes an in-depth look at planning and managing the Foundation Stage. There is discussion of the principles which should underpin planning, a detailed section on content, experiences and resources, advice on managing the provision and on including adults and the community, and guidance on ensuring quality.

Rich in detail about how to plan and implement activities that address children's learning. Nursery World

The **First Hand Audit** is a practical guide to writing a policy for the Early Years and includes an easy-to-use audit for reviewing your own provision.

Foundations for Independence ISBN 1 902233 57 3
We Can Do It! ISBN 1 904187 79 X

by Sally Featherstone & Ros Bayley

These popular books provide clear guidance for supporting independent learning in young children. **Foundations for Independence** looks at the value of independent learning and describes how practitioners can plan and resource the early years in order to create the conditions for children to develop into self-motivated, autonomous learners. **We Can Do It!** addresses 8 aspects of learning. Each is carefully explained, so that you can use it to ensure independent learning is at the heart of your setting. The emphasis is on practical help, and good use is made of examples and case studies in a full colour, practical handbook.

Beautifully set out and delightfully easy to follow. Early Years Specialist, Hants.

Very important, up to date and relevant ... I enjoyed reading this thought-provoking book. Foundation Stage Teacher.

Smooth Transitions ISBN 1 904187 67 6

by Ros Bayley & Sally Featherstone

The tensions between Reception and KS1 have now been acknowledged. This book offers advice for teachers, practitioners, parents and managers on supporting children through the move from the Foundation Stage to Yr 1. Includes a special section on using new knowledge about how children learn.

This is brilliant! I want every infant teacher in Britain to have a copy. Sue Palmer, Educational Consultant

Practical....accessible....invaluable. It will help you do what we all know is right for the children. Early Years Educator Magazine

Inside Out

ISBN 1 904187 27 7

by Sally Featherstone with Anne Cummings

How to plan and organise a range of role play situations, inside and out. Part 1 discusses why role play is important and Part 2 presents plans for a range of role play situations. There are ideas for materials, equipment and locations, including making the most of limited resources. Unlock your imagination and help your children to bring out what's inside!

Cooking Up A Story

ISBN 1 905019 00 9

by Mary Medlicott

A wonderful collection of stories and storytelling advice from a leading children's storyteller. The emphasis is on creativity and enjoyment - getting children engaged and using their imaginations. The sound, practical guidance for practitioners will help even the least confident to make the most of storytime. Delightfully illustrated in full colour by Martha Hardy.

Images of Violence

ISBN 1 9050109 15 7

by Sîan Adams & Janet Moyles

In the aftermath of September 11th 2001 the authors noticed new features creeping into children's play. These appeared to be reflecting the extensive media coverage of acts of terrorism and violence, from the attacks on the World Trade Centre to bombings in Bali and Madrid and the invasions of Afghanistan and Iraq. Their impressions were confirmed by discussion with early years practitioners and further observations and led them to reflect on some key issues for those who work with young children.

Through a series of case studies and a review of the literature on children and violence the authors reflect on children's responses to the images of violence they see, and seek to provide help for practitioners in dealing with some of the educational and social problems they present.

Timely, welcome and refreshing. Times Educational Supplement

Available by mail order from the publisher, or from your usual book supplier.

**Featherstone Education PO Box 6350 Lutterworth LE17 6ZA
United Kingdom**
T:(+44 0)185 888 1212   F:(+44 0)185 888 1360
sales@featherstone.uk.com www.featherstone.uk.com